Community Bank Strategic Lending Choices and Performance

Gary Whalen

OCC Economics Working Paper 2007-3

July 2007

Community Bank Strategic Lending Choices and Performance[*]

Gary Whalen

Abstract

Most community banks have been unable to increase dramatically the percentage of their revenue coming from non-traditional sources and so remain reliant on the net income generated by traditional intermediation activities. This continued dependence means that the lending strategy chosen by any community bank is a key determinant of its survival. In this study the lending strategies chosen by a sample of 5508 community banks are examined over the 1995 – 2004 period. Links among the chosen strategies, strategic change, and performance are also investigated using both univariate and regression analysis. The analysis of lending strategy trends reveals an increase in the percentage of community banks that emphasize lending to business borrowers and a decrease in the fraction of institutions specializing in loans to non-commercial customers. The data also indicate that the typical community bank changed its lending strategy over the decade, and many did so more than once.

Differences in performance are evident across the strategic groups. The results indicate that business real estate lenders earned the highest returns over the decade, but also were the riskiest. When returns are adjusted for risk, a number of lending strategies produced performance exceeding that of business real estate lending, including residential real estate lending, diversified lending, and agricultural lending. The results show that strategic change reduces returns and increases risk, all else equal. The evidence indicates a large performance disadvantage for the smallest community banks regardless of the lending strategy they pursue.

JEL Classification: G21, L21, L25

Keywords: Community banks, lending strategy, real estate, risk, return

[*]The opinions in this paper are those of the author and do not necessarily reflect those of the Office of the Comptroller of the Currency or the Treasury Department. The author would like to thank David Nebhut for comments on an earlier draft and Amy Millen for editorial assistance.

Please direct any comments to Gary Whalen, Senior Economic Advisor, Office of the Comptroller of the Currency, 250 E St., SW, Washington, DC 20219, gary.whalen@occ.treas.gov or (202) 874-4441.

I. Introduction

Since the early 1990s the twin forces of deregulation and technological change have combined to intensify the competitive pressure on all banks.[1] These pressures are reflected in the steady substantial decline in the total number of banking firms and a sharp increase in the aggregate share of industry output concentrated in the hands of the largest banking organizations.[2] This ongoing industry consolidation has motivated a fair amount of empirical research on bank performance as researchers have sought to explain this structural trend and its implications. A number of these studies have focused on the performance of community banks, because small locally oriented banking companies play a crucial role in providing relationship-based loans to opaque borrowers.

Generally, these studies reveal that community banks are either unwilling or unable to embrace non-traditional strategies and continue to rely much more heavily on portfolio lending and intermediation income than larger banks in the current environment.[3] This means that the most important strategic choice community bank management must make is the kind(s) of traditional lending business to pursue. In particular, should they emphasize a particular type of lending or broadly diversify their loan portfolio? And, if they decide to specialize, what type of lending specialty should they choose? Which, if any, lending strategy produces the highest risk-adjusted return?

There has been virtually no work investigating the alternative lending strategies chosen by community banks or the impact of those strategies on their performance. This paper attempts

---

[1] For a good description of the changing environment for banks over time, see DeYoung, Hunter and Udell (2004).
[2] Tables 1 and 2 in Critchfield, et.al. (2004) illustrate these structural trends.
[3] The continued heavy emphasis on traditional portfolio lending by community banks rather than noninterest income is documented in DeYoung and Rice (2004A) and DeYoung and Rice (2004B).

to remedy that deficiency. In this study, the strategic lending choices of a sample of 5508 community banks are examined over the 1995 – 2004 period. Links between chosen lending strategies, the frequency of strategic change, and performance are also investigated using univariate and regression analysis.

The analysis of lending strategy trends reveals an increase in the percentage of community banks that emphasize lending to business borrowers and a decrease in the fraction of institutions specializing in loans to non-commercial customers. The data also indicate that the typical community bank changed its lending strategy over the decade, and many did so more than once.

Alternative lending strategies are associated with differences in performance. The results indicate that business real estate lenders earned the highest returns over the decade examined. But there is also evidence that community banks specializing in this sort of lending were the riskiest. When returns are adjusted for risk, a number of lending strategies produced performance exceeding that of business real estate lending, including residential real estate lending, diversified lending, and agricultural lending. The results also illustrate the importance on controlling for other factors when examining the relationship between lending strategies and performance. One important factor is the extent to which community banks changed their lending strategies. Another important factor that must be controlled for in the analysis is community bank size. The results show that more frequent strategic change reduces returns and increases risk, all else equal. The evidence indicates a large performance disadvantage for the smallest community banks regardless of the lending strategy they pursue. The paper also provides some evidence that a simultaneous equation framework should be employed when the linkage between strategy and performance is explored.

II. Previous Studies Examining Bank Strategic Choice and Associated Performance Effects

Relatively few empirical studies have examined the strategic choices made by community banks in recent years and related impacts on performance. The most notable relevant papers are Stiroh (2004), Hirtle and Stiroh (2005), Eisenbeis and Kwast (1991), and Blasko and Sinkey (2006).

Stiroh (2004) investigates the performance effects of differences in bank loan portfolio composition and diversification for a sample of roughly 4500 community banks over the 1984-2000 interval.[4] He uses four broadly defined loan portfolio share variables (total real estate, commercial and industrial, consumer and all other) and the related Herfindahl-Hirschman Index (HHI) diversification measure, HHI_{LOAN}, averaged over his sample period to capture bank lending strategies.[5] Measuring lending strategy in this way might be problematic for several reasons. First, the loan share variables, especially the real estate share, are defined broadly. Residential and commercial real estate loans are likely to have different risk/return characteristics and combining them into a single share variable could alter the magnitude, sign, and statistical significance of the estimated effects of the strategy indicators and performance. Second, using multi-year averages of the lending strategy variables in the analysis provides no insight on the extent of any changes in strategy over his lengthy sample period. There is some evidence that the typical bank changes its lending strategy over much shorter time horizons. The failure to control for strategic change could alter the observed effects of differences in loan portfolio composition and diversification on performance.

---

[4] He also examines revenue diversification as well.
[5] HHI_{LOAN} is the sum of the squares of four loan portfolio shares: real estate loans, commercial and industrial loans, consumer loans, and other loans.

Descriptive statistics for the loan strategy variables do show that loan portfolio composition and diversification varies considerably across his sample of community banks.[6] For example, the mean value of the real estate loan portfolio share for his sample banks is 46.6 percent, with a standard deviation of 17.3 percent. The mean and standard deviation of the HHI_{LOAN} value are 0.42 and 0.10, respectively, with sample values ranging from 0.26 to 0.99.[7] The mean HHI_{LOAN} value suggests that the loan portfolio of the typical community is not broadly diversified.[8]

Because lending strategy potentially influences bank risk and return, Stiroh estimates variants of three basic performance equations using ordinary least squares (OLS). The dependent variables in the sets of estimated equations are risk-adjusted return on equity (ROE), risk-adjusted return on assets (ROA), and the Z-score, respectively.[9] The set of explanatory variables includes three of the loan portfolio share variables, the diversification variable $HHI_{LOAN,}$ and a limited number of other control variables as well. The real estate loan share is omitted to avoid multicollinearity. This specification means that the coefficients on the included loan share variables measure their impact on performance relative to real estate loans.

The regression coefficients on the variable HHI_{LOAN} are negative and significant in all three of the risk-adjusted return equations estimated, implying that increased loan portfolio diversification is associated with improved performance. He also typically finds negative significant coefficients on the three included loan portfolio composition variables. These results mean that risk-adjusted performance tends to fall as community banks increase the share of non-

---

[6] See Stiroh (2004), table 2, p. 144.
[7] The maximum value of any HHI is 1.0.
[8] Given his decision to split loan portfolios into four loan types, equal portfolio shares imply an HHI_{LOAN} value of 0.25.
[9] The risk-adjusted profitability measures are formed by dividing a given measure of mean profitability by the related standard deviation. The Z-score is an inverse indicator of risk. The numerator of the Z-score is the sum of mean ROA and the mean value of the ratio of equity divided by assets. The denominator is the standard deviation of ROA.

real estate loans in their portfolios. Since the excluded loan share represents the most important type of lending activity, Stiroh concludes that the negative coefficients on the included loan portfolio composition variables imply that community bank performance suffers when the banks move away from areas where they have the most expertise and experience.

Hirtle and Stiroh (2005) investigate the extent to which banking organizations have adopted more retail-oriented strategies in recent years and the impact of this sort of strategic change on their performance. More specifically, they attempt to determine if retail banking is less risky and more profitable than alternatives like wholesale banking or less-traditional fee-based lines of business. Their sample is an unbalanced panel consisting of 3110 annual observations for 708 bank holding companies of all sizes over the years 1997-2004.

They develop four different retail strategy indicators in their paper, but the most relevant for the current study is their estimate of the share of each company's total loan portfolio represented by "retail" loans.[10] Like the loan share variables used by Stiroh, their retail loan definition combines a variety of loan types in the numerator that are likely to have very different risks and returns.[11]

Unlike Stiroh, they construct and analyze annual retail strategy measures for each company over the sample period. Prior to their statistical analysis, they examine trends in the level of the retail loan share variable over the 1993-2004 period for several groups of different sized holding companies. They find different movements in this lending strategy ratio when they compare small and the largest companies. The retail loan share was highest at the smallest companies at the outset of the period, roughly 15 percentage points above that of the largest

---

[10] They create a similar retail indicator based on deposits and a third by dividing branch offices by total assets. The fourth indicator is a composite constructed using principal components analysis.
[11] It includes credit card loans, other consumer loans, residential mortgages (including home equity), and small commercial and industrial loans.

banks. Over the interval the retail loan share of small companies steadily declined. Conversely, the retail loan ratio began to rise in 2000 for the largest companies, and this strong upward trend continued through 2004. By the end of the period, the largest holding companies had the highest retail loan share of any size group, exceeding that of small companies by more than 10 percentage points.

To test their main hypothesis, they estimate OLS regressions of holding company rates of return, return volatility, and risk-adjusted rates of return for a given year on their measure of retail banking activity and other control variables lagged one year. They estimate each type of performance regression using both an accounting-based and market-based version of the respective dependent variable.[12] The use of annually measured strategy data in their performance regressions instead of multi-year averages provides some evidence on the effects of changing strategy over time. But the use of single one-year lag between the retail strategy variables and the performance measures may be too short and simple to show clearly the true relationship between the two.

A large number of performance equations are reported in the paper. These regressions include six different dependent variables, different sets of the strategy variables, and are estimated using the complete and three size-based sub-samples. Since the results are generally consistent across the alternative specifications, only the estimated equations with market-based dependent variables generated using the complete sample are discussed here.

When stock market returns are used as the dependent variable in the estimated performance regressions, the estimated coefficient on the retail lending indicator is negative and significant, implying that higher levels of retail lending activity are associated with lower

---

[12] The risk adjusted return variable is either a market-based or accounting measure of return divided by a comparable measure of the standard deviation of returns.

returns. Increases in retail lending significantly reduce risk in the regression where the market-based measure of return volatility is used as the dependent variable. In the equation where a risk-adjusted market return measure is used as the dependent variable, the estimated coefficient on the retail lending measures is also negative and significant implying worse performance for banking companies with a greater emphasis on retail activities.[13]

The coefficients on several of the non-strategy control variables included in the estimated equations to capture other potentially important information about the rest of the loan portfolio are also of interest. The shares of total loans represented by non-retail commercial and industrial loans and all other loans are two such variables.[14] As in Stiroh (2004), a loan portfolio HHI concentration measure is also included on the right-hand side.

The two loan share variables are both insignificant in the market return equations. The coefficient on the commercial loan share is positive and significant when market return volatility is used as the dependent variable. The other loan share variable has a negative significant effect on risk-adjusted market returns.

The estimated coefficient on the loan portfolio HHI is positive in all of the versions of the market return equation and is significant in a majority of cases. This result implies more concentrated loan portfolios are associated with higher returns. In the market return volatility and the risk-adjusted return equations, the estimated coefficient on the portfolio concentration measure is also positive and typically significant. Taken together, these results imply that companies with more concentrated loan portfolios have higher and more volatile returns and on net, better risk-adjusted performance.

---

[13] The three equations are equation (1) in tables 3,4, and 5, respectively.
[14] The omitted loan share variable is thus non-retail real estate loans divided by total loans.

Eisenbeis and Kwast (1991) examine the performance of banks that chose to specialize in real estate lending over the 1978-1988 time period. They separate their sample of all insured commercial banks in each year into two groups based on the percentage of their assets represented by all loans secured by real estate. This is the same sort of overly broad strategic characterization used in Stiroh (2004) when no distinction is made between residential and non-residential real estate loans. They classify banks with total real estate loans-to-assets (TREL) ratios of 40 percent or more at a given year-end as real estate lending banks (REBs) for that year. The 40 percent cutoff value was chosen subjectively. The authors also create a sub-group of long-term real estate lending specialists because they observe that banks change their lending strategy over time and expect that the performance of banks persistently following a real estate lending strategy might differ from other banks. They place banks in this sub-group if they met the REB definition in 5 or more of the 11 years of the sample period (5REB). Banks that do not qualify as REBs and that pass a number of additional screens form the control group of banks in each year.[15]

They find substantial variation in the percentage of sample banks classified as REBs over time. At the outset of the period examined, 6.8 percent of their sample is in the REB category. This percentage declines steadily to a low point of 1.5 percent in 1983 and increases each subsequent year to 10.4 percent in 1988. The fraction of the sample represented by 5REB banks also varies over time, but is quite small in all years, never exceeding 2 percent.

Eisenbeis and Kwast use call report data to construct a large number of performance measures for their sample banks in each year. They compare summary statistics (typically means) for each performance indicator for the REB and 5REB groups to that of their control

---

[15] In each year, banks are excluded from the control group if their asset size exceeds that of the largest REB in the sample, or if they had 0 real estate loans, or if they converted from an S&L charter in the previous three years. They also exclude any bank (including REBs) that had extreme ROA values.

group banks each year and use univariate tests to determine if any observed differences are statistically significant.

Their analysis of differences in measures of overall return and risk are of primary interest. They use mean ROA as their return proxy and the standard deviation of ROA as their primary indicator of risk.[16] They find significant differences in mean returns between REB and 5REB banks and their control group of banks in most years over their sample period. But the nature of the return difference changes fundamentally over the 11 year interval. From 1978 through 1982, the two groups of real estate banks are less profitable than non-real estate lenders. In the last half of the period, real estate banks are more profitable than control group banks and the largest and statistically strongest differential is evident for the 5REB group. In fact, the profitability of the 5REB group is higher than the REB group in almost every year, suggesting that consistent pursuit of this lending strategy produced the best returns over this particular time period.

They also find significant differences in return variability in almost every year between both groups of real estate lending banks and the control group. In 10 years (seven significant), return variability for the REB group is below that of non-real estate lending banks. A similar and more pronounced risk difference is evident for 5REB banks. The ROA standard deviation for 5REB banks is significantly below that of the control group in all years and all of the differences are significant. And in every year, this indicator shows that 5REB banks are less risky than REB banks.

---

[16] See table 2, p.10. They also present Z score risk measures for the three groups of banks in table 2, but these figures are constructed from the aggregate risk, return, and equity capital ratios for each group that appear in the table rather than from bank-level data. As a result, it is not possible to statistically test for significant differences between the three groups of banks.

Eisenbeis and Kwast also investigate asset and loan portfolio composition differences across their three groups of sample banks over time to try to identify more precisely the sources of the observed differences in risk and return. One important persistent significant difference they find is that both REB and 5REB banks have much higher loan-to-asset ratios (LAR) than control group banks.[17] They note that these LAR differences are one reason why real estate specialists were more profitable than the non-real estate banks. The correlation between the LAR variable and the lending strategy indicator reveals the potential benefits of a multivariate approach and explicitly controlling for LAR differences in this sort of analysis.

When they examine differences in the real estate portfolios of their sample banks, Eisenbeis and Kwast find that 1-4 family residential real estate loans account for the bulk (more than 50 percent) of the real estate loans at all three groups of banks in all of the years examined.[18] While the statistical tests lead to a rejection of the null hypothesis that the mean ratios are the same at real estate and non-real estate banks, the percentage point differences in shares across the three groups of companies are relatively small. Nonfarm, nonresidential loans represent the second largest share of real estate loans at all three groups of banks, accounting for roughly a quarter of total real estate loans. Examination of the trends in shares of the various types of real estate loans over the 11 year period, however, reveal a considerable increase in the percentage of real estate loans represented by commercial real estate credits in the portfolios of both REB and 5REB banks.[19] This sort of compositional change could alter the relative performance of the three groups of banks and will not be reflected when total real estate loan holdings are used to categorize lending strategy.

---

[17] See table 5, panel A, p.16. In 1988 the difference is roughly 14 percentage points.

[18] See table 5, panel B, p. 17.

[19] For example, the mean share of total real estate loans represented by nonfarm nonresidential loans was roughly 10 percentage points higher in 1988 than it was in 1978 at REB and 5REB banks. The change in construction loan share was about 5 percentage points.

Finally, Eisenbeis and Kwast investigate changes in the real estate loan-to-asset ratio over time at banks that are classified as REB in various time periods to gain insight on the speed and magnitude of adjustments in strategy.[20] They find that REBs changed their real estate loan concentration substantially and relatively quickly over time. This evidence on changes in strategy suggests that examining the relationship between annual measures of performance and lending strategy might not be informative.

Blasko and Sinkey (2006) adopt the basic approach of Eisenbeis and Kwast to investigate the relationship between bank real estate lending and performance during the 1990s. They use the same ratio (total real estate loans divided by total assets) and cutoff value (40 percent) to separate their sample of all insured commercial banks each year from 1989 through 1996 into real estate lending banks (REB) and the control group of banks (non-REB). They split REB banks into two categories each year based on their REB status over the entire period. One of these sub-groups consists of banks that met the REB definition in four or more of the eight years of the sample period (REB4+). The other sub-group (REB1-3) consists of banks that met the REB definition in one, two, or three years over the eight year period.

They find that the percentage of all banks represented by REBs more than doubled over the eight-year period examined, rising from 13.6 percent in 1989 to 29.8 percent in 1996. Over the same period, REB4+ banks went from 9.7 percent of all banks to 18.7 percent. In all years the average size of the REB4+ banks is relatively small and is well below that of the non-REB group. In six of the eight years, the differences in mean size are statistically different.

---

[20] See table 6, p. 19.

Their analysis primarily focuses on the impact of this portfolio shift on bank risk. They use several different equity capital ratios and the Z-score as alternative indicators of risk.[21] Univariate t-tests reveal if there are significant differences in mean values of their alternative risk indicators at non-REBs vs. REB1-3 and REB4+ in each year. They find that mean capital ratios are lower at both groups of REBs than they are at non-REBs in every year examined and that the differences are generally statistically significant suggesting that REBs tend to be riskier.

Their analysis of differences in mean Z-scores at the three groups of banks over time, however, yields results that are somewhat at odds with those based on capital ratios. They do find mean Z-scores are lower in every year at REB1-3 banks than they are for non-REBs, indicating that the former are riskier than the latter. These differences are also statistically significant. But this pattern is not apparent for the REB4+ banks. In fact, mean Z scores for the REB4+ group are higher than they are at non-REB banks for the first four years of the period, and in three years the differences are significant. In six of the eight years, the mean Z scores of the REB4+ banks exceed those of the REB1-3 group. Neither of these patterns constitutes strong support for the notion that REBs are substantially more risky than non-REBs.

They also estimate two simple OLS regressions using the Z-score as the dependent variable. In the first version, the key explanatory variable is the ratio of total real estate loans divided by total assets. In the second, a dummy variable is used as the measure of a bank's real estate exposure. This variable takes on a value of one for REB banks and otherwise is set equal to zero. The equations also include only return on assets, a size variable, and year and regional dummies as additional control variables. The estimated coefficients on the real estate lending

---

[21] They analyze differences in equity divided by total assets, the total risk-based capital ratio, and the Tier 1 risk-based capital ratio. They use six previous ROA values to calculate the Z score for each sample bank in each year.

variables are negative and significant in both equations, indicating that banks more heavily involved in real estate lending tend to be more risky, all else equal.

They also explore differences in accounting rate of return measures between the two groups of real estate lending banks and non-REB banks over time to a limited extent.[22] They find that mean ROA for the REB1-3 group is below that of the non-REB control group in all eight years, and the difference is significant in six years. The mean ROA of REB1-3 banks is also below that of REB4+ banks in every year. Mean ROA for the REB4+ group is higher than that of the control group in four of the years examined. In two of these years the difference in mean returns is significant. The differences in mean returns are significant in all four of the years when REB4+ banks under-perform the control group.[23]

Like Eisenbeis and Kwast they find that real estate lenders have much higher loan-to-asset ratios than non-REB banks in every year examined.[24] As in the earlier study, the majority of real estate loans at REB1-3 and REB4+ banks are 1-4 family residential loans, but there is some evidence of increased commercial real estate lending at REB4+ banks over the eight-year period.

The empirical studies typically find significant relationships between a variety of different lending strategy measures and bank risk and return. Much of the evidence relates to the performance effects of real estate lending, and the real estate strategy measure is defined very broadly and possibly imprecisely in all cases. Evidence also reveals substantial and quick changes in lending strategy over time, supporting a focus on the relationship between longer-term strategy and performance measures in this type of analysis. None of the studies explicitly

---

[22] Table 5, p. 67.

[23] The results are more mixed when ROE is used as the return measure because ROE reflects differences in both ROA and leverage.

[24] The difference is more than 15 percentage points in 1989 and 1996. See table 7, p.71.

explore the performance effects of strategic change. The substantial correlations found between strategy indicators and other bank characteristic variables that could have separate, significant effects on performance suggest that multivariate statistical techniques should be used.

III. Data Issues

III.a. The Community Bank Sample

The initial sample was drawn from the set of all banks in operation at least three full years as of year-end 1994 and that subsequently survived through the end of 2004. Banks are retained in the sample if they met a community bank definition similar to that used in previous studies. Sample banks had to have total assets less than $1 billion as of year-end 2004. Multibank holding company affiliates are included only if the largest affiliate of their holding company also met this same size constraint. Community banks are retained in the final sample if they pursued one of the seven most common lending strategies over the 1994-2004 time period. The process of assigning banks to these groups is discussed as follows. This procedure yields a sample of 5508 banks for analysis.

III.b. Lending Strategy Definitions

There are a number of different ways to classify the lending strategies of banks. Since all such classification schemes are inherently subjective, an existing simple methodology developed at the OCC is employed in this paper.[25] In this approach community banks are initially placed

into one of 10 strategic peer groups each quarter on the basis of differences in the composition of

their asset portfolios.[26] More specifically, a series of percentage-of-asset ratios that reflect the

types of lending done by community banks are used to represent each bank's portfolio

composition at the end of each quarter. All of the ratios are constructed from call report data.

For each bank, these asset composition ratios are ranked from highest to lowest value.

Generally, a bank is assigned to a particular strategic lending group if its largest portfolio share

represents that type of lending, if the largest portfolio share represents at least 25 percent of total

assets and if the largest share is at least 10 percentage points above the asset share represented by

the second most important type of lending. This classification scheme places most banks in

seven strategic lending groups: residential real estate lending, household lending, diversified

lending, business lending, business real estate lending, agricultural lending, and no-specialty

lending.[27] The classification procedure is described in detail in the appendix.

Like any subjective strategic classification scheme, this method has advantages and

disadvantages. On the plus side, the classification procedure is available, is relatively

straightforward, and results in reasonable characterizations of alternative lending strategies. The

classification algorithm reflects the relative importance of all of the types of lending done by

each bank and so is likely to produce more homogeneous strategic groupings than alternatives

that use a single or an array of more broadly defined asset share ratios.

However, the set of ratios and the cutoff values used to make the strategic classifications

are chosen judgmentally. The set of ratios used to make the classifications also does not reflect

---

[25] The FDIC uses a similar procedure to place banks into "specialization groups."

[26] Banks that have been in operation for less than three years are placed in an eleventh de novo category.

[27] Banks defined here as diversified lenders are actually labeled business and household lenders in the OCC classification scheme. The name was changed to reduce possible confusion of banks in this group with those defined to be business lenders or household lenders.

potentially important dimensions of lending strategy that influence risk and return. For example, the ratios used to place banks in the residential lending peer group do not reflect differences in the risk of mortgages (credit or interest rate) banks hold in their portfolio. They also do not reflect differences in the degree to which banks engage in secondary mortgage market activities.

Although the peer group classifications are available quarterly, in this paper the lending strategy of each bank is only measured at each year-end to simplify the analysis. Intra-year changes in lending strategy are ignored. The use of annual lending strategy classifications means that strategic change could be understated in the analysis to some extent. This approach also amounts to an implicit assumption that bank performance for a particular year reflects the strategy it had in place at the end of that year. This assumption complicates the empirical analysis of any link between strategy and performance if strategic change is common, because the quarter in which banks alter strategy during a year is not observed. As a result the time a given strategy has been in place after a change is imprecisely measured and could weaken any relationship between a given strategy and performance.

Admittedly the use of annual strategic classifications entails pitfalls. But observing strategies annually over a decade allows the identification of any predominant strategy as well as the measurement and exploration of strategic change.

IV. Trends in Community Bank Lending Strategies 1995 – 2004

The analysis begins with an examination of trends in community bank lending strategies over the 1995 – 2004 time period. A useful starting point is to compare the percentages of sample institutions that fall into each peer group classification at the beginning and at the end of the period of observation. These two snapshots are reflected in chart 1. The left hand bar for each peer group depicts the percentage of sample banks that fell into that group at year-end 1994. The right hand bar shows the percentage at the end of 2004. The first two peer groups on the horizontal axis, residential real estate lending and household lending, represent banks that lend primarily to retail customers.

The first bar shows that the most popular strategy at the outset of the period was residential real estate lending, with roughly 30 percent of all community banks falling into that peer group. About 10 percent of sample banks were household lenders in 1994. The chart shows that the percentage of banks in both of these groups declined considerably by the end of the period. At the end of 2004, roughly 20 percent of banks were classified as residential real estate lenders and only 4 percent were household lenders. Conversely, the percentages of banks in the three peer groups that focus more heavily on business lending generally increased over the period. In 2004, the most popular lending strategy was diversified lending, with 22 percent of all banks falling into this category vs. 20 percent at the start of the period. Business real estate lending was almost as popular in 2004, accounting for 18 percent of sample banks, a striking 15 percentage point increase compared to 1994. Roughly 17 percent of sample banks pursued business lending strategies at this time, up 4 percentage points over the decade.

The percentage of banks in the remaining two strategic lending categories declined slightly over the period. The fraction of banks in the agricultural lending group declined several percentage points from 14.5 percent in 1994 to about 12 percent in 2004. The percentage of community banks classified as no-specialty lenders also declined from 9.0 to 5.5 percent over the decade.

Looking at the peer group classifications at only the two endpoints of the period provides limited insight on the direction and frequency of changes in lending strategies by community banks over time. More detailed evidence on strategic change by the community banks over the decade is contained in tables 1 through 3.

Table 1 shows the extent to which community banks adopt a "primary" lending strategy, here defined as a lending strategy pursued for at least six years over the period. Banks that do not pursue any lending strategy for at least six years are considered to have no primary strategy. The concept of a primary lending strategy facilitates empirical analysis of the relationship between strategy and performance given the possibility of strategic change. If a bank follows a given primary strategy, its performance will reflect this strategy for at least the majority of years over the decade of observation, and the nature of any relationship should be evident in long run indicators of its risk and return. In addition, banks that change strategy can be included in the analysis, and the performance effects of strategic change can be explored.

The numbers in each of the first seven rows of table 1 are the percentage of banks in each 1994 strategic group that pursued each of the various primary lending strategies or did not adopt any primary strategy. To illustrate, the first entry in the first row of table 2 shows that 57.99 percent of banks that were residential real estate lenders in 1994 made this their primary lending strategy over the entire period. The 2.57 percent figure in the second column of the first row represents the percentage of banks that were residential real estate lenders at the outset of the period but had a primary lending strategy of household lending over the 10-year period of observation. The figure in the last column of the first row gives the percentage of 1994 residential real estate lenders that did not have a primary lending strategy over the complete period. The percentages along the diagonal of table 1 provide insight on the extent to which

18

banks stuck with their initial strategies. The off-diagonal percentages illustrate the nature and duration of the strategic lending changes made by community banks. Generally, the data indicate considerable changes in lending strategy by community banks over the period.

The last row of the table shows the percentage of community banks in the entire sample with each possible primary lending strategy, or again none at all. These figures paint a slightly different picture of community bank lending strategies over the decade than is conveyed by the two snapshots depicted in chart 1. The most popular primary strategy over the entire period is residential real estate lending, accounting for 21.97 percent of all banks in the sample. The next highest percentage, 21.77 percent, represents the percentage of sample community banks that did not have any identified primary lending strategy. Only 6.5 percent of the sample banks fall into the business real estate primary strategy group. This finding, in conjunction with the relatively large percentage of sample banks pursuing this strategy in 2004, suggest that the obvious trend in this direction is relatively recent and possibly reflects opportunistic behavior by banks that have pursued alternative lending strategies over portions of the past decade.

The analysis of primary strategies in table 1 provides only a crude picture of the frequency of strategic changes by community banks over time. A more direct measure of the frequency of strategic change is the total number of different lending strategies pursued by each bank over the decade. This information is presented in table 2. Each cell of the first seven rows of the table shows the percentage of banks in each 1994 strategic group that followed a given number of different lending strategies over the decade. This first entry in the first row of the table shows that 31.17 percent of banks initially in the residential real estate lending group never deviated from this strategy over the entire period. The last entry in the first row indicates that 1.47 percent of the initial group of residential real estate lenders ultimately pursued more than

19

four different lending strategies over the period. The figures in the last row of table 2 are the percent of all sample banks that followed each possible number of lending strategies over the period. The numbers reveal that only 23.33 percent of the sample banks followed a single lending strategy consistently over the 10 year period, while roughly a third of the sample had three of more different lending strategies. The mean value of the number of different lending strategies pursued for the complete sample is 2.25; the median value is 2.0.

An alternative measure of the frequency of strategic change is the total number of times a bank changed strategic lending groups over the decade. This sort of metric captures the behavior of banks that pursued a limited number of strategies but alternated between them over time. Table 3 presents the same sort of information on the number of strategic lending changes for banks in each 1994 strategic class as contained in table 2. In fact, the first columns of each table are the same because by definition banks that follow a single strategy do not change their lending strategy over the period. Like the data in table 2, the percentages in table 3 show that most banks change strategy over time. The figures in the last row of the table indicate that 58 percent of sample banks changed strategy at least twice over the decade and 38 percent did so three or more times.

Table 4 contains selected data that illustrates how different the banks in the alternative primary lending strategy groups are from one another. The first nine rows of the table contain mean values of variables that reflect potentially important differences in the loan portfolio composition of the sample banks.[28] Average size and age are reported in the next two rows. The final variable in table 4 reflects the extent of strategic change by banks in each primary lending group.

---

[28] The loan portfolio composition measures in the table are not necessarily the same ones used to make the lending strategy classifications.

Generally the mean values of the loan portfolio share variables reveal the expected differences across the lending groups given the classification scheme. For example, the mean value of the residential real estate loan share variable is much higher for banks in the residential real estate primary lending group than it is for banks pursuing other strategies. But the extent to which banks concentrate on the type of lending that characterizes its primary lending strategy group does differ across the groups. Examining the mean values of the loan portfolio share variables and the loan portfolio HHI reveals that business real estate lenders and agricultural lenders tend to be the most specialized, while diversified lenders tend to be the least specialized. But the data in the table also show that banks in each of the lending strategy categories make considerable amounts of loans that are not their specialty as well.

Considerable differences in the mean values of the loan-to-asset ratio are also evident across the lending strategy groups in the table. These differences are potentially important in the empirical analysis because they might have a separate influence on performance that should not be attributed to primary lending strategy.

The average size of banks also varies quite a bit across the groups. The average asset size of business real estate lenders is $206 million, almost four times larger than the average agricultural lender ($56 million). These differences are also potentially important since previous research has shown that size has an important impact on community bank performance.

The mean values of bank age show little differences across the strategy groups with one exception. Business real estate lenders have been in operation for much less time than banks in the other strategic categories. This finding indicates that this is a popular strategy for recently chartered banks.

21

The last row of the table 4 contains the mean value of the number of different lending strategies pursued by the banks in each primary lending strategy category. Some variation is evident across the groups with agricultural lenders and residential real estate lenders changing strategy the least. Not surprisingly, those banks without a primary strategy changed lending strategy the most.

V. Strategy and Performance

The primary focus of this paper is to determine if and how community bank lending strategies influenced their risk and return. A related issue of interest is the performance impact of strategic change. As noted previously, difficulties arise in empirical explorations of these relationships if strategy is observed annually and strategic change is common because the quarter in which banks that actually made the change is ignored. The time a given strategy has been in place is potentially important because there may be a lag between the adoption of the strategy and related impacts on performance. Given possibly imperfect measurement of the timing of strategic change, exploring the relationship between annual measurements of strategy and annual measures of performance is not likely to be productive. Dropping the substantial number of banks that change strategy from the analysis would reduce the sample considerably and preclude any exploration of the impact of strategic change.

The approach taken here is to examine empirically the relationship between primary lending strategies and long run measures of performance. The performance of a sample bank measured over the 10-year period of observation should reflect any primary lending strategy since by definition it has followed that strategy for at least a majority of years over that interval.

In addition, banks that change strategy can still be included in the analysis, and the performance effects of strategic change can also be explored.

The same standard ex post risk and return measures used in previous work are employed here. All of the performance measures are derived from accounting data contained in the Reports of Income and Condition all banks must file with regulators. The return measure for each bank is mean annual pre-tax rate of return on equity (MEANPTROE) calculated over the 10-year span beginning in 1995 and ending in 2004.[29] The risk measure is the standard deviation of the annual return on equity measure (SDPTROE) calculated over the same 10-year period.[30] In some of the analysis, a Sharpe ratio (SHARPE) is used as a measure of risk-adjusted return. The numerator of the Sharpe ratio is the mean of the difference between the pre-tax return on equity in each year and the corresponding average return on a one-year constant maturity Treasury bill over the 10-year period. The denominator is SDPTROE. Risk-adjusted return measures like the Sharpe ratio reflect both the risk and return associated with each strategy and permit strategies with different combinations of risk and return to be compared and evaluated. In particular, this sort of risk-adjusted return measure can reveal whether higher return strategies that also entail higher risk are superior to lower-risk, lower-return strategies.

These long-run performance measures can be calculated only for banks that operated over the entire 1995 – 2004 interval, and so only "surviving" banks are included in the sample. Using such a sample can influence the empirical findings. For example, banks that pursued the riskiest strategies may have been more likely to disappear over the decade-long time period, and this may bias the measured returns of these strategies upward and/or risk downward.

---

[29] Comparisons are made using pre-tax ROE to minimize the effects of Subchapter S status on profitability. A considerable number of community banks have chosen this form over the sample period.
[30] Extreme values of MEANPTROE and SDPTROE are also winsorized at the 1st and 99th percentile values.

V. a. Univariate Analysis

Table 5 contains the mean values of the three performance variables for sample banks that pursued each of the alternative primary lending strategies over the 1995-2004 period.[31] In addition, mean values are also included for sample banks that did not follow any primary lending strategy. The first four columns in the table contain data for all sample banks. Because previous research has shown that size influences bank performance and could also be correlated with lending strategy, the mean values of the three performance variables examined here are also reported separately for small community banks (2004 total assets less than $100 million) and large community banks (2004 total assets greater than $100 million and less than $1 billion) in the two other panels of the table.

Looking at average returns for the complete sample of banks in column two of the table, the most profitable primary strategy over the period is business real estate lending with a MEANPTROE value of 18.09 percent. This value is roughly two percentage points higher than that of the second most profitable strategy of diversified lending with a mean value of 16.11 percent. Residential real estate lending ranks third with a mean return of 15.07 percent, followed by business lending at 14.89 percent. The three primary lending strategies with the lowest mean returns are agriculture which ranks sixth with a MEANPTROE value of 14.00 percent, household lending at 13.77 percent, and no-specialty lending which was the least profitable strategy at 11.32 percent.

The mean return for banks with no primary lending strategy is fifth highest at 14.60 percent. This finding does not necessarily mean that strategic change has a relatively modest

---

[31] Univariate analysis of median values of the performance variables did not materially change any of the reported conclusions and so are not reported.

24

performance impact because the number of strategic changes made by banks in this category varies considerably and the performance of banks in this class reflects an unknown mix of lending strategies. A more carefully constructed analysis designed to provide evidence on the performance effects of strategic change is discussed later.

The next column of the table shows the mean values of the risk variable, SDPTROE, for each of the primary strategic classifications. Risk is highest for banks that engaged primarily in business real estate lending with a mean SDPTROE value of 5.80 percent. The second highest value of the risk variable (4.92 percent) is observed for banks that did not have any primary strategy, followed by household lenders at 4.60 percent, diversified lenders at 4.54 percent, business lenders at 4.48 percent, agricultural lenders at 4.16 percent, residential real estate lenders at 3.77 percent, and no-specialty lenders at 3.52 percent.

The values in the fourth column of table 5 are the mean Sharpe ratio values for all banks in each primary lending strategy category. Residential real estate lending yielded the best risk-adjusted returns for the period with a mean Sharpe ratio of 4.14, slightly above the second-best value of 4.00 for banks that had a primary strategy of diversified lending. The mean ratio for the business real estate lending strategy of 3.65 ranks third indicating that banks engaged in this activity must take high risks to earn high returns. Business lending ranks fourth with a mean Sharpe ratio of 3.46 followed by banks with no primary strategy (3.39), agricultural lenders (3.38), household lenders (3.32), and no-specialty lenders (2.60). The risk-adjusted return rankings of the alternative strategies are roughly similar to that based on unadjusted returns, but do differ in two cases. Residential real estate lending switches performance rankings with business real estate lending when returns are adjusted for risk, rising from third best to first. This shift occurs because the lower risk of residential real estate lending more than offsets the lower returns of this activity. Formal statistical tests reveal that the differences between the mean Sharpe ratio for residential real estate lenders and each of the other peer group means except diversified lenders are statistically significant.

The data in the two additional panels of table 5 for small and large community banks reveal the influence of bank size on the analysis of strategy returns and risks. Comparing mean return and risk values for the two size classes of banks for every lending strategy shows that in every case except one, small community bank returns are lower and risk is higher than they are for large community banks. The average return advantage for large community banks across the eight lending strategies is nearly 350 basis points. The mean return for the least profitable strategy for large community banks is only slightly below the mean return of the most profitable small bank lending strategy. The comparable risk advantage is roughly 75 basis points. The combined effects of the return and risk disadvantages for small community banks explain why their mean Sharpe ratios or risk-adjusted returns are lower than large banks for every type of strategy. Clearly size has an influence on performance independent of strategy. These results suggest that failure to control for size when investigating the risks and returns of alternative strategies may lead to incorrect conclusions about the source of observed performance differentials. This is particularly true when the proportion of small community banks pursuing each strategy differs considerably, as is the case here.

The ranking of mean lending strategy returns for small community banks differs relative to the results for the complete sample. Diversified lending is the most profitable strategy for small community banks with a mean return of 14.58 percent, followed by business real estate (13.89 percent), business (13.56 percent), residential real estate (13.49 percent), agriculture (13.41 percent), household (12.98 percent), no primary strategy (12.66 percent), and non-

26

specialty lending (10.33 percent). The risk rankings of the alternative lending strategies for small community banks also differ from that for the whole sample, but the differences are somewhat less than is the case for returns. Business real estate lending again is the riskiest lending strategy, diversified lending ranks second, no primary strategy is third, followed by household lending, business lending, agriculture, residential real estate, and no-specialty lending. The different rankings in strategy returns and risk combine to produce several notable differences in the ranking of risk-adjusted returns for small community banks relative to that of the complete sample. Residential real estate lending remains the strategy with the best risk-adjusted returns, and diversified lending continues to rank second best. But agricultural lending becomes the strategy with the third-highest risk-adjusted returns, while small community banks that specialize in business real estate lending have the lowest mean Sharpe ratio.

The most profitable strategy for large community banks is business real estate lending with a MEANPTROE value of 18.84 percent. The large community bank lending strategy with the second-highest return (17.36) is diversified lending. Agricultural lending is the third-most profitable lending strategy for large community banks. Large community banks with no primary strategy had the fourth-best returns, followed by business lenders, and residential real estate lenders. The two least profitable strategies for large community banks are household lending and no-specialty lending with mean returns of 15.66 and 14.42 percent, respectively.

The riskiest lending strategy for large community banks is business real estate lending, the same as it is for small banks. Large community banks without a primary lending strategy have the second-highest mean SDPTROE value, followed by business lenders, household lenders, diversified lenders, no-specialty lenders, and agricultural lenders. The least risky lending strategy for large community banks is residential real estate lending.

The ranking of large community bank lending strategies based on risk-adjusted returns is generally similar to the one for small community banks. As is the case for small community banks, residential real estate lending has the highest risk-adjusted returns, diversified lending ranks second with agricultural lending in third place. Large community bank household lenders have the fourth-best mean Sharpe ratio, followed by business lenders and banks without any primary strategy. Large community banks that are business real estate lenders have the seventh best risk-adjusted returns. Large no-specialty lenders have the lowest mean Sharpe ratio.

The data in table 6 provide insight on the performance effects of strategic change. To discern the effects of strategic change, it is necessary to control for differences in primary strategy since the previous analysis has shown that choice of primary strategy influences risk and return. Each panel of table 6 shows the means for the same three performance variables for subgroups of banks that followed a given primary strategy where subgroup membership depends on the number of different lending strategies followed by a given bank over the decade. Three different strategic change classifications are created for each primary lending strategy. The first consists of banks that never deviated from their primary lending strategy over the entire decade. The second subgroup for each primary lending strategy consists of banks that followed at least two different lending strategies over the period. Banks in the third subgroup for each primary lending strategy pursued three or more different strategies.

In general, the data in table 6 show that more frequent strategic change is associated with lower returns (both unadjusted and risk-adjusted) and higher risk for all of the major primary lending strategies. For all six of the primary lending strategies examined, mean unadjusted returns are higher for banks that followed a single lending strategy over the decade than for either of the comparison subgroups of banks that changed strategy more frequently. In addition, in every case the subgroup that followed three or more different strategies had the lowest mean unadjusted returns. For five of the six primary strategies, examination of the mean SDPTROE values also shows that banks that did not change strategy were less risky than both of the comparison subgroups of banks that did change strategy. Since the Sharpe ratios depend on the level and volatility of returns, it is not surprising that the observed relationship between these measures of risk-adjusted returns and the frequency of strategic change is identical to that observed for unadjusted returns. For every lending strategy, banks that did not change strategy have the highest level of mean risk-adjusted returns.

A number of alternative explanations exist for these findings. One is that the number of different strategies pursued is a signal of management quality. Less capable managers may be less likely to identify and implement a winning strategy. Another possibility is that strategic change tends to be costly. Still another explanation is that poor performance motivates managers to change strategy.

VI. Regression Analysis

The univariate analysis provides some insight on the relationships between lending strategy, size, and community bank performance. But these findings may reflect the influence of a number of other variables that affect performance, lending strategy, or both that cannot be explicitly controlled for when a simple univariate approach is employed. Regression analysis provides better estimates of the separate influences of lending strategy and a broader set of factors on community bank risk and return.

Several versions of a return equation and a risk equation are estimated in this study. In each specification of the return equation, mean annual pre-tax return on equity (MEANPTROE) over the 1995-2004 period is the dependent variable. In the risk equation, the dependent variable is the standard deviation of annual pre-tax ROE (SDPTROE) measured over the same period.

In both the return and risk equations, seven dummy variables are used to represent the alternative primary lending strategies of the sample banks: residential real estate lenders (RESRED), household lenders (HHD), diversified lenders (DIVD), business lenders (BUSD), business real estate lenders (BUSRED), agricultural lenders (AGD), and no-specialty lenders (NOSPLD). Thus, banks that did not pursue one of these primary lending strategies form the omitted reference group in each equation, and the estimated dummy variable coefficients reflect the performance impact of each primary strategy relative to banks without one. Since the paper focuses on the impact of lending strategy on performance, all of the reported regression equations include the entire set of seven dummies as explanatory variables even if their associated coefficients are not statistically significant.

The other explanatory variables that appear in the reported versions of the return and risk equations reflect the results of previous empirical work, preliminary analysis of alternative specifications and judgment. Four different specifications of the return and risk equations are reported in tables 7 and 8, respectively. The simplest specification appears in the first column of each table and includes the seven primary lending strategy dummies and a basic set of additional control variables. The second specification of each performance equation adds a measure of the extent to which each bank changed lending strategy over the period to the set of explanatory variables because the univariate analysis suggests that the frequency of strategic change affects both risk and return. The total number of different lending strategies (NUMLENDSTRAT) pursued by sample banks over the observation period is used as the measure of strategic change. The third specification for each performance equation drops NUMLENDSTRAT and adds the other performance variable to the basic set of explanatory variables to provide insight on possible simultaneity.[32] Previous research suggests that a simultaneous equations framework is appropriate in empirical studies of the determinants of bank risk and return.[33] The fourth specification adds both the strategic change indicator and the other performance measure to the basic set of right-hand-side variables. The definitions of all of the variables appearing in the estimated equations along with their means and standard deviations appear in table 10.

Linear regression (OLS) is used to estimate each of the equations in tables 7 and 8. The reported standard errors in the tables are White-corrected. Following the practice of earlier studies, banks that had not been in operation for at least 10 years as of year-end 1995 were excluded from the estimation sample to lessen the likelihood that the results reflect the behavior of immature institutions.

VI. a. The Return Equations

Examination of the regression coefficients on the lending strategy dummies and the associated test statistics in the four versions of the estimated return equation reported in table 7 reveal only a few lending strategies whose returns consistently differ significantly from those of the reference group of banks that did not follow a primary lending strategy. In particular, the addition of the strategic change measure to the set of explanatory variables has a material impact on the estimated coefficients on the primary lending strategy dummies as well as their statistical

---

[32] So in the third specification of the return equation, the risk measure (SDPTROE) is included as an explanatory variable and vice versa.
[33] See Berger and Bonaccorsi di Patti (2006), Clark (1986), and Liang (1989), for example.

significance. The strongest result is apparent for business real estate lenders. In all four specifications the coefficient on BUSRED is positive and is significant in three, including the last equation, with both the strategic change and risk variable included as explanatory variables. Banks following this primary lending strategy earned significantly higher returns than the reference group banks. Using the coefficients from equation 4 in table 7 the mean pre-tax return on equity of business real estate lenders is roughly 9.8 percent higher than that of the typical no-primary strategy bank.[34]

While the lending dummy coefficients and associated t-statistics do not reveal consistent significant differences between each of the primary lending strategy groups and the reference group of banks, the regression results can also be used to test whether returns differ significantly across the seven different primary lending groups. This is accomplished by testing whether or not the seven estimated coefficients on the primary lending strategy groups are all equal to one another. This hypothesis can be rejected for all four of the reported return equations, which means that returns do differ significantly across the seven different primary strategies. The hypothesis that the coefficients on the residential real estate lender dummy and the business real estate lender dummy are equal to one another is also rejected in all four regressions. This result supports the separation of real estate lenders into two separate groups in the analysis of the effect of lending strategy on performance.

The remaining explanatory variables in the return equations that are of the greatest interest are the strategic change variable NUMLENDSTRAT and the risk measure SDPTROE. The estimated coefficient on NUMLENDSTRAT is negative and significant in both of the specifications in which it appears. This is consistent with the results of the univariate analysis

---

[34] Using average estimation sample values for the non-dummy variables, predicted returns are 14.44 percent for business real estate lenders vs. 13.15 percent for reference group banks.

32

that showed that banks that changed lending strategy more often earned lower returns. As noted previously, a number of plausible explanations exist for this sort of relationship. The negative relationship between changes in lending strategy and profitability might reflect differences in management quality, the costs of strategic change, or reverse causation.

The estimated coefficient on the risk variable SDPTROE is also negative and significant in both of the return equations in which it is included. This result is somewhat surprising. Managers are typically assumed to be willing to take additional risk only if they are compensated with higher expected returns. The observed negative relationship could reflect the effects of unobserved differences in management quality. Risk will be higher and returns lower at poorly managed banks. Another possibility is that the result reflects the inappropriate use of OLS to estimate a return equation that should properly be viewed as part of a system in which risk and return are simultaneously determined. The identical result reported in three previous studies that advocate the use of a simultaneous equation approach when investigating bank performance supports this interpretation.[35] Subsequent analysis presented as follows does reveal that the estimated coefficient changes considerably when risk and return are treated as jointly determined.

The signs and statistical significance of the other explanatory variables used in the return equations are not a primary concern in this study and so will be discussed only briefly. The estimated coefficient on the state charter dummy (STATEBANK) is positive and significant, indicating state banks were more profitable than national banks over this period. This could reflect higher explicit supervisory fees paid by national banks. The coefficient on the size variable (LOGASSET) is also positive and significant in line with expectations and consistent with the results of the univariate analysis and previous empirical work. This finding may reflect

---

[35] This result is reported in Clark (1986), Liang (1989), and Berger and Bonaccorsi di Patti (2006).

33

the existence of scale economies. The estimated coefficient on the core deposit variable (NONMATDEPR) is also positive and significant, suggesting that core deposits are less costly than purchased funding. The results also show that banks with higher loan-to-asset ratios (LOANASSETR) are significantly more profitable all else equal. This is not surprising since the yields on loans are generally higher than those obtainable on short term investments or securities.

The estimated coefficient on the Subchapter S corporation dummy (SUBCHAPS) is positive and significant in all of the return equations. This means that Subchapter S banks were more profitable even on a pre-tax basis than conventionally organized C corporations. The explanation for this finding is not clear, but it could be attributable to control advantages resulting from more concentrated ownership.[36] The coefficient on the multibank holding company affiliate dummy (MBHCD) is also positive and significant. This result probably reflects cost savings stemming from affiliation with a larger consolidated organization.

The coefficient on the bank's weighted local market deposit share (MKTSHARE) is also positive and significant. This result could either reflect the impact of market competition or efficiency. Some researchers have argued that higher market share permits the exercise of market power which results in higher profitability. Others take the position that market share is a proxy for firm efficiency. More efficient firms gain market share and are more profitable. Since measuring the impact of competition is not the focus of this study, no attempt is made to resolve this ambiguity.[37]

---

[36] The maximum number of shareholders in Subchapter S corporations is restricted. The American Jobs Creation Act of 2004 increased the maximum to 100 from the previous cap of 75.

[37] In some studies that investigate the relationship between market structure and profitability, a measure of market concentration is also included in the estimated equations. In this study, the profitability equations were also estimated with a concentration measure used in place of the market share term and with both variables included. Collinearity was problematic when both variables were used. When the two variables were used one at a time, the results were generally similar (positive, significant coefficients), but were somewhat stronger when market share was employed and so this specification was adopted.

The final two explanatory variables reflect conditions in the local markets in which the sample banks operate. The positive significant coefficient on the average annual weighted local market deposit growth variable (MKTDEPGR) is reasonable. Profitability is higher for banks operating in more rapidly growing, economically robust local markets. The negative significant coefficient on the variable measuring the percentage of local market deposits controlled by savings institutions (SLMKTDEPR) is also not surprising. Bank profitability should be lower in markets with more thrift competition.

VI. b. The Risk Equation

In contrast to the relatively weak relationships between the different primary lending strategies and profitability revealed in the return equations, somewhat stronger, more consistent relationships are evident when risk is the dependent variable in the performance regression. The estimated coefficient on the business real estate lending dummy is positive and significant in all four versions of the risk equation reported in table 8, indicating that the risk associated with this lending strategy is significantly greater than that of the reference group banks. Again using mean values for all of the non-dummy variables in equation 4 in table 8, the predicted risk of a business real estate lending strategy is roughly 25 percent higher than that of banks that did not have any primary lending strategy.[38]

The estimated coefficients of two other primary lending strategy dummies, residential real estate lending and agricultural lending are negative and significant in all four specifications, indicating less risk than that of the reference group banks. As is the case for business real estate lenders, the magnitudes of the coefficients imply considerable differences in risk relative to no-

---

[38] The predicted standard deviation of pre-tax ROE is 5.55 vs. 4.426 for reference group banks.

primary strategy banks. The predicted risk of residential real estate lenders is 13.6 percent below that of the reference group banks. The risk of agricultural lenders is 15.1 percent lower.[39]

Given the evidence of consistent significant differences in risk associated with three of the primary lending strategies and the opposing signs of the associated coefficients, it is not surprising that the hypothesis that all seven estimated coefficients on the primary lending strategy groups are all equal to one another can also be rejected for all four of the risk regressions. It is also possible to reject the hypothesis that the risk of residential and business real estate lenders is the same. These results show that there are significant differences in the risk associated with the alternative primary lending strategies even when the effects of other potential explanatory variables are controlled for in a regression framework.

As was the case in the return equations, the strategic change variable NUMLENDSTRAT has a significant impact on risk in both of the specifications in which it appears. In this case, however, the estimated coefficient on NUMLENDSTRAT is positive which means that banks that change lending strategy more often tend to be riskier, all else equal. This is the same result found in the simpler univariate analysis. Managers that change lending strategy more often may possess less information on their borrowers or be less skillful loan underwriters than managers that never, or rarely, change strategy.

When the profitability measure is used as an explanatory variable in the risk equation, the estimated coefficient is negative and significant in both of the equations in which it is included. One possible explanation is management quality. Superior management produces higher returns and is also better at controlling risk. Another related explanation is that well-managed banks possess a persistent efficiency advantage, resulting in higher profitability and franchise value.

---

[39] The predicted risk values are 3.822 and 3.758, respectively using mean values of non-dummy explanatory variables in equation 4 of table 8.

Higher franchise value serves to mitigate risk-taking behavior.[40] In any event, the addition of profitability as an explanatory variable in the risk equation does not materially change the estimated impacts of the different primary lending strategies on risk, at least when the equation is estimated separately using linear regression techniques.

Other explanatory variables are included in the risk equations. Some of those variables appear in the return equations, others do not. Again, the impacts of those variables on bank risk are a subsidiary issue and are discussed only briefly.

The estimated coefficient on the state charter dummy is negative and significant, indicating that state banks were less risky than national banks over this period. The reason for this finding is not clear. The coefficient on the size variable is negative and significant in the risk equation. This result presumably reflects the effects of a size-based diversification advantage. Higher loan-to-asset ratios are associated with significantly greater risk. This is reasonable since loans are generally less liquid and have greater credit risk than other types of bank earning assets. The negative significant coefficient on the equity-to-asset ratio (EQUITYASSETR) indicates higher capital ratios are associated with lower risk. The coefficient on the noninterest income variable (NONINTINCR) is positive and significant, in line with the results reported in previous work. The positive significant coefficient on the loan growth variable (LOANGROWTHR) is consistent with the notion that banks that grow faster tend to be riskier. The HHI variable LHERF is an inverse measure loan portfolio diversification. The positive significant coefficient indicates banks with less diversified loan portfolios are more risky, all else equal. The estimated coefficient on the MBHC affiliate dummy is also positive and significant, indicating that these banks tend to be more risky than one bank holding company

---

[40] The determinants of bank franchise value and its impact on risk-taking have been explored in a number of papers. See Berger and Bonaccorsi di Patti (2006) and Demsetz, Saidenberg, and Strahan (1996).

affiliates or independent banks. This result may reflect perceived or actual diversification advantages attributable to affiliation with a larger consolidated entity.

The last explanatory variable in the risk equations is the standard deviation of annual weighted market deposit growth (SDMKTDEPGR) over the 1995-2004 period. This variable is intended to capture differences in the volatility of economic conditions in the local markets in which each sample bank operated during the interval examined. More variable economic conditions in local markets should be reflected in more variable market deposit growth rates, increasing the riskiness of banks that operate there. The positive significant coefficient is consistent with this expectation.

VI. c. Considering Simultaneity in Risk and Return

If risk and return are determined jointly in a simultaneous system, OLS estimates of the impacts of the explanatory variables in the risk and return equations will be biased and inconsistent.[41] Several existing studies cited previously provide theoretical and empirical support for the use of a simultaneous equations framework, although the sets of endogenously determined and control variables differ.[42] Statistical testing confirmed that the return and risk measures appearing in the estimated equations should be treated as endogenous variables.[43]

---

[41] See the discussion in Clark (1986), pp. 296-297.
[42] Clark (1986) estimates a four equation system where the endogenous variables are mean ROE, the standard deviation of ROE, mean total loans divided by total assets and mean total time and savings deposits divided by total liabilities. Liang (1989) estimates a two equation system where mean ROA and the standard deviation of ROA are the endogenous variables. Berger and Bonnaccorsi di Patti (2006) estimate a two equation system where the endogenous variables are a measure of profit efficiency and the ratio of equity divided by total assets. They use the standard deviation of return on equity as their risk measure and assume that it is an exogenous variable in both of these equations.
[43] The test described in Davidson and MacKinnon (1993), pp. 236-242 was used.

Given the lack of consensus on a single correct specification, several different versions of the risk and return equations presented in tables 7 and 8 are re-estimated as systems using two-stage least squares (2SLS) to reveal whether accounting for simultaneity materially alters the empirical results. The results are presented in table 9.

Two different two-equation systems are estimated. The first system of equations (Model A) in table 9 consists of equation (3) from tables 7 and 8. The second (Model B) consists of equation (4) from tables 7 and 8. The only difference between the two is that Model B includes the measure of strategic lending changes as an explanatory variable in both of the equations while Model A does not. In general, the performance effects of the alternative lending strategies are similar to those observed when the risk and return equations are estimated individually using OLS. Comparing the primary lending strategy coefficients in the two models confirms the importance of controlling for strategic change in the analysis. For example, four of the lending strategy dummy variable coefficients are significant in the return equation in Model A, but none remain so in the Model B specification. Three lending strategies significantly influence risk in both the Model A and Model B specifications. Business real estate lenders are significantly more risky than the reference group of banks, while the opposite is true for residential real estate and agricultural lenders. The 2SLS estimates also reveal the existence of significant feedback between risk and return in Models A and B. The return variable has a negative significant coefficient in the risk equation, the same result found in the OLS estimation. The coefficient on the risk variable is also significant in the return equation, but the sign is positive, the opposite of the result obtained when the equation OLS was used to estimate the equation. The positive coefficient is consistent with a priori expectations.

Finally, since the univariate analysis revealed that lending strategies were systematically related to differences in loan-to-asset ratios and this variable was treated as endogenous in a previous study, a three-equation system (Model C) was also estimated to examine the impact of this additional change in specification on the previously reported impacts of the alternative lending strategies. Model C consists of the risk and return equations of Model B plus a third equation where the dependent variable is the loan-to-asset ratio. In addition to the set of lending strategy dummies, the loan-to-asset ratio is assumed to depend on bank charter type, asset size, market deposit growth, the frequency of lending strategy change, and risk.

Adding this third equation to the system does alter the signs and statistical significance of several of the coefficients on the lending strategy dummies in the return equation, relative to Model B where the loan-to-asset ratio is assumed to be exogenous. Household and no-specialty lenders are significantly more profitable than the no-primary strategy reference group when Model C is estimated. Diversified lenders and agricultural lenders are significantly less profitable than reference group banks in the three equation system.

Generally, the signs and statistical significance of the other explanatory variables in the return equation are not materially different in Model C vs. Model B. The one exception is the reduction in the significance of the negative coefficient on the measure of the frequency of strategic change. This result reflects the indirect impact of strategic change on returns through the loan-to-asset ratio that is revealed in the third equation of Model C.

Endogenizing the loan-to-asset ratio has less of an impact on the sign and significance of the estimated coefficients on the explanatory variables in the risk equation than it does in the return equation. The same three lending strategy dummies found to be significant in Model B retain their significance in Model C with unchanged signs. Business real estate lenders are again found to be more risky than the reference group of no-strategy banks, while the opposite is true for residential real estate lenders and agricultural lenders. The estimated effects of the other explanatory variables on risk are basically the same in Model C as they are in Model B.

Turning to the third equation in Model C, the results show that loan-to-asset ratios differ substantially at banks with different lending strategies. Banks in three primary lending categories – diversified lending, business real estate lending, and agricultural lending – had loan-to-asset ratios significantly above the reference group of no-strategy banks. The opposite result was found for household lenders, business lenders, and no-specialty lenders.

The signs and significance of the coefficients on the other explanatory variables in the loan-to-asset equation appear to be reasonable and are discussed briefly since they are not of primary interest here. State chartered banks had significantly higher loan-to-asset ratios all else equal. This effect may reflect higher legal lending limits for state chartered banks in some states over the period. The results show that larger banks tend to have higher loan-to-asset ratios. Loan-to-asset ratios also are higher at banks that operate in more rapidly growing local markets. Banks that change lending strategy more often have significantly lower loan-to-asset ratios. And finally, more risky banks have higher loan-to-asset ratios, all else equal.

VII. Summary and Conclusions

Over the past decade, the operating environment of community banks has become more difficult. Most have been unable to increase dramatically the percentage of their revenue coming from non-traditional sources and so remain reliant on the net income generated by traditional intermediation activities. This continued dependence means that the lending strategy chosen by any community bank is a key determinant of its survival. Yet few researchers have investigated recent trends in community bank lending strategies and the relationship between lending strategies and performance.

In this study the lending strategies chosen by a sample of 5508 community banks are examined over the 1995 – 2004 period. Links among the chosen strategies, strategic change, and performance are also investigated using both univariate and regression analysis. The analysis of lending strategy trends reveals an increase in the percentage of community banks that emphasize lending to business borrowers and a decrease in the fraction of institutions specializing in loans to non-commercial customers. The percentage of sample banks specializing in commercial-oriented lending rose from 30.8 percent in 1994 to 46.9 percent in 2004, while the corresponding percentage of consumer lenders fell from 40.3 to 25.8.[44] The data also indicate that the typical community bank changed its lending strategy over the decade, and many did so more than once.

Differences in performance are evident across the strategic groups. However, these findings are difficult to characterize definitively because they depend on the performance measure examined, the type of statistical analysis employed, and the specification of the performance equations when regression analysis is used. The results indicate that business real estate lenders earned the highest returns over the decade examined. But there is also evidence that community banks specializing in this sort of lending were the riskiest. When returns are adjusted for risk, a number of lending strategies produced performance exceeding that of business real estate lending including residential real estate lending, diversified lending, and agricultural lending. The results also illustrate the importance of controlling for other factors when examining the relationship between lending strategies and performance. One important

---

[44] Here business-related lenders include business lenders, business real estate lenders, and agricultural lenders. Consumer lenders include residential real estate lenders and household lenders.

factor is the extent to which community banks changed their lending strategies. The results show that strategic change reduces returns and increases risk, all else equal. Another important factor that must be controlled for in the analysis is community bank size. The evidence indicates a large performance disadvantage for the smallest community banks regardless of the lending strategy they pursue. These results support the use of regression analysis when investigating the performance effects of alternative lending strategies. The paper also provides some evidence that a simultaneous equation framework should be employed when the linkage between strategy and performance is explored.

Further research on community bank strategy and performance is warranted. Alternative, more comprehensive measures of strategy could be developed. Here the strategy and strategic change variables are assumed to be exogenous. They may depend on a number of factors including risk and return. The regression analysis reveals that the results are somewhat sensitive to the specification employed and so the robustness of the reported findings should be examined using reasonable alternatives. It might also be useful to reexamine this issue as more recent data become available, since they may be time-period specific.

Appendix

Details on the Lending Strategy Classification Procedure

The algorithm used to make the peer group classifications at the end of each quarter uses the following variables:

Bank Age (AGE): Number of years a bank has been in operation.

Foreign Asset Ratio (FORAR): Total foreign assets divided by total assets.

Securitized Credit Card Asset Ratio (SCCAR): Total securitized credit card assets divided by total assets.

Loan Asset Ratio (LAR): Total gross loans divided by total assets.

Credit Card Loan Ratio (CCLR): Total credit card loans divided by total assets.

Residential Real Estate Loan Ratio (RESRELR): Total mortgage backed securities + loans secured by 1-4 family residential properties + other real estate owned secured by 1-4 family residential properties divided by total assets.

Agricultural Loan Ratio (AGLR): Agricultural production loans + loan secured by farmland divided by total assets.

Business Real Estate Loan Ratio (BRELR): Construction loans + loans secured by multifamily properties + loans secured by nonfarm, nonresidential properties + loans secured by real estate held in foreign offices + other real estate owned not secured by 1-4 family properties divided by total assets.

Other Consumer Loan Ratio (OCRLR): Other consumer loans divided by total assets.

Commercial Loan Ratio (COMLR): Commercial and industrial loans divided by total assets.

Other Commercial Loan Ratio (OCOMLR): Loans to state/local governments + all other loans + loans to depositories + leases + loans to foreign governments divided by total assets.

Retail Loan Ratio (RETLR): Mortgage-backed securities + loans secured by 1-4 family residential properties + total consumer loans + other real estate owned secured by 1-4 family residential properties divided by total assets.

Wholesale Loan Ratio (WSLR): AGLR + BRELR + COMLR + OCOMLR.

The bank population is first run through four filters. Banks with AGE < 3 are assigned to the "de novo" peer group. Banks with FORAR values of 25 percent or more are classified as "international banks." Those with SCCAR values of 25 percent or more are classified as "credit card banks" and banks with LAR values below 10 percent are defined as "nonlenders."

The following ratios for remaining unclassified banks are then ranked from highest to lowest value: CCLR, RESRELR, AGLR, BRELR, OCRLR, COMLR and OCOMLR. If the largest ratio for a bank is greater than or equal to 25 percent and exceeds the second largest ratio by 10 percentage points or more, it is assigned to a peer group using the following set of rules. If the largest ratio for the bank is CCLR, it is classified as a "credit card bank." If RESRELR is the largest ratio, it is classified as a "residential real estate lender." Banks whose largest ratio is AGLR are classified as "agricultural lenders." If BRELR is the largest ratio, the bank is labeled a "business real estate lender." Those where OCRLR is the largest ratio are categorized as "household lenders." "Business lenders" are banks where COMLR or OCOMLR is the largest ratio.

The ratios RETLR and WSLR are examined for banks that remain unclassified. If RETLR and WSLR both are greater than or equal to 25 percent, the bank is defined to be a "diversified lender." If RETLR meets the 25 percent threshold and WSLR does not, the bank is classified as a "household lender." If the opposite is true, the bank is considered to be a "business lender." And, if the bank still remains unclassified and its LAR value is at least 10 percent, it is labeled a "no-specialty lender."

References

Berger, A. and E. Bonaccorsi di Patti. (2006). Capital Structure and Firm Performance: A New Approach to Testing Agency Theory and an Application to the Banking Industry. *Journal of Banking and Finance* 30, 1065-1102.

Blasko, M. and Joseph F. Sinkey. (2006). Bank Asset Structure, Real-Estate Lending, and Risk-Taking. *Quarterly Review of Economics and Finance* 46, 53-81.

Clark, J. (1986). Single-Equation, Multiple-Regression Methodology: Is It an Appropriate Methodology for the Estimation of the Structure-Performance Relationship in Banking? *Journal of Monetary Economics* 18, 295-312.

Critchfield, T., T. Davis, L. Davison, H. Gratton, G. Hanc and K. Samolyk. (2004). The Future of Banking in America Community Banks: Their Recent Past, Current Performance, and Future Prospects. *FDIC Banking Review* 16 No. 3, 1-56.

Davidson, R. and J. MacKinnon. (1993). *Estimation and Inference in Econometrics.* New York: Oxford University Press.

Demsetz, R., M. Saidenberg, and P. Strahan. (1996). Banks With Something To Lose: The Disciplinary Role of Franchise Value. Federal Reserve Bank of New York *Economic Policy Review* 2 No.2, 1-14.

DeYoung, R. and T. Rice. (2004A). How Do Banks Make Money? The Fallacies of Fee Income. Federal Reserve Bank of Chicago *Economic Perspectives* 28 Fourth Quarter, 34-51.

DeYoung, R. and T. Rice. (2004B). Noninterest Income and Financial Performance at U.S. Commercial Banks. *Financial Review* 39, 101-127.

DeYoung, R., W. C. Hunter, and G. Udell. (2004). The Past, Present, and Probable Future for Community Banks. *Journal of Financial Services Research* 25 no. 2-3, 85-133.

Eisenbeis, R. and M. Kwast. (1991) Are Real Estate Specializing Depositories Viable? Evidence From Commercial Banks. *Journal of Financial Services Research* 5, 5-24.

Hirtle, B. and K. Stiroh. (2005). The Return to Retail and the Performance of U.S. Banks. Federal Reserve Bank of New York Staff Report No. 233.

Liang, N. (1989) Bank Profits, Risk, and Local Market Concentration. *Journal of Economics and Business* 41, 297-305.

Stiroh, K. (2004) Do Community Banks Benefit From Diversification? *Journal of Financial Services Research* 25 Nos. 2-3, 135-160.

Chart 1
Percent of Community Banks in Each Lending Strategy Peer Group: 1994 vs. 2004

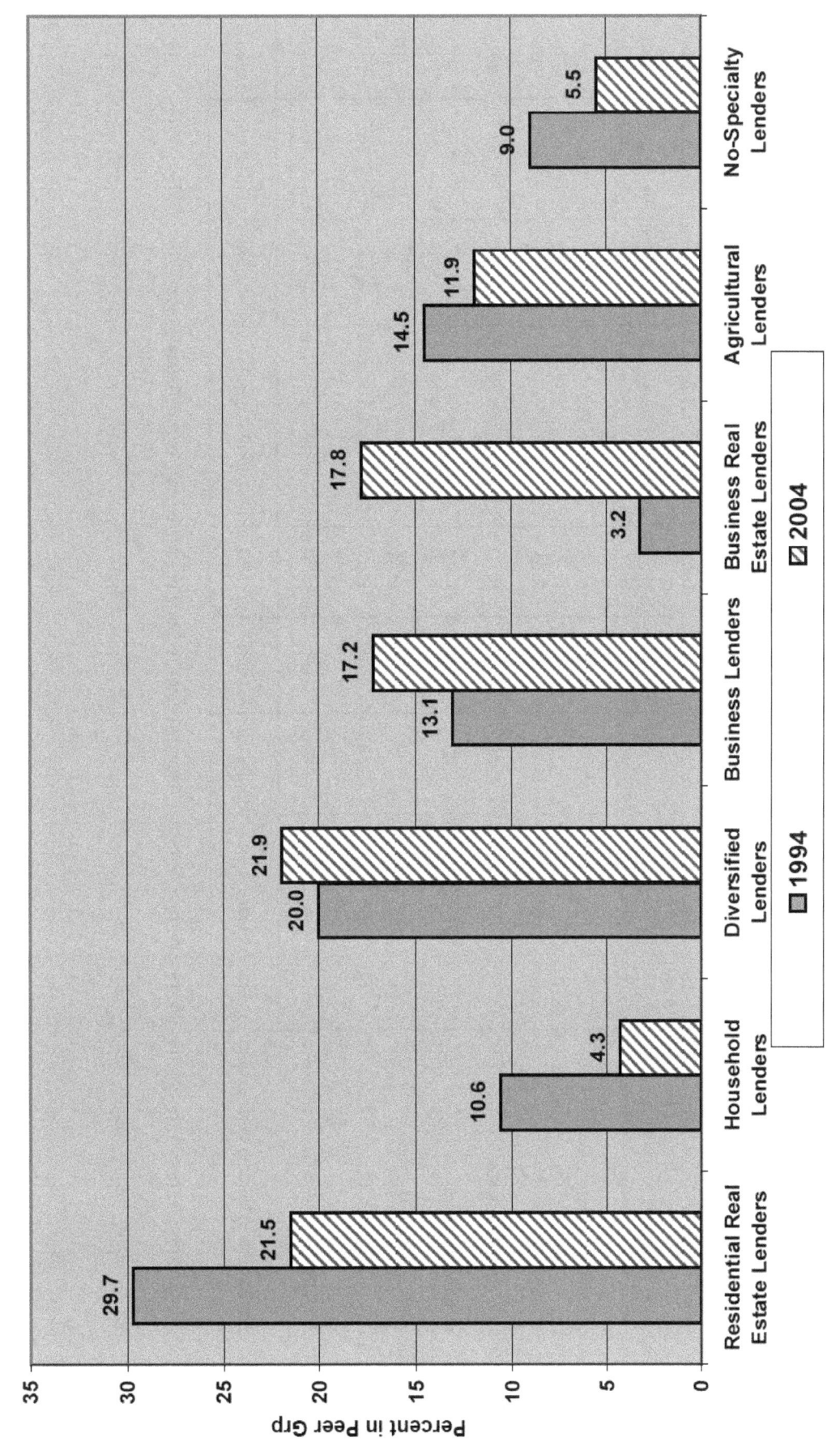

Table 1

Percent of Initial Lending Strategy Peer Group in Each Primary Lending Strategy Peer Group[*]

1994 Lending Strategy Peer Group	Primary Lending Strategy Peer Group							
	Residential Real Estate	Household	Diversified	Business	Business Real Estate	Agricultural	No-Specialty	None
Residential Real Estate Lenders	57.99	2.57	12.86	1.96	1.35	0.24	0.92	22.11
Household Lenders	19.97	31.91	13.31	2.73	1.88	0.17	3.41	26.62
Diversified Lenders	8.34	1.90	45.15	10.61	7.80	2.90	0.00	23.30
Business Lenders	0.83	0.00	10.43	44.23	12.24	9.04	2.64	20.58
Business Real Estate Lenders	0.57	0.00	4.57	2.86	81.14	0.00	0.00	10.86
Agricultural Lenders	0.13	0.00	5.40	7.78	0.38	74.28	0.00	12.05
No-Specialty Lenders	9.29	5.05	3.84	14.14	0.81	0.81	33.33	32.73
Percent of Total Sample in Primary Peer Group	21.97	4.99	16.90	11.26	6.46	12.67	3.98	21.77

[*] A bank is placed in a particular primary peer group if it was classified with that lending strategy in 6 or more years over the 1995-2004 period.

Table 2

Percent of 1994 Lending Strategy Peer Group vs. Number of Different Lending Strategies

1994 Lending Strategy Peer Group	Number of Different Lending Strategies				
	1	2	3	4	>4
Residential Real Estate Lenders	31.17	33.25	25.11	9.00	1.47
Household Lenders	7.68	41.47	35.15	13.31	2.39
Diversified Lenders	8.07	51.41	34.54	5.44	0.54
Business Lenders	12.66	49.65	30.46	6.82	0.42
Business Real Estate Lenders	49.14	32.57	14.29	4.00	0
Agricultural Lenders	49.56	31.37	16.69	2.38	0
No-Specialty Lenders	14.14	27.68	32.73	21.01	4.44
Percent of Total Sample	23.33	39.11	27.89	8.42	1.25

Table 3

Percent of 1994 Lending Strategy Peer Group vs. Number of Changes in Lending Strategies

1994 Lending Strategy Peer Group	Number of Lending Strategy Changes						
	0	1	2	3	4	5	>5
Residential Real Estate Lenders	31.17	16.04	21.13	14.15	10.10	5.08	2.33
Household Lenders	7.68	24.23	22.01	20.31	10.75	8.02	6.99
Diversified Lenders	8.07	23.12	21.40	21.40	15.05	6.80	4.16
Business Lenders	12.66	23.50	17.94	19.89	16.13	6.12	3.76
Business Real Estate Lenders	49.14	1.14	25.14	8.57	9.14	4.57	2.28
Agricultural Lenders	49.56	15.56	15.18	9.41	5.40	3.01	1.88
No-Specialty Lenders	14.14	12.53	21.62	19.80	16.57	8.48	6.87
Percent of Total Sample	23.33	18.45	20.17	16.65	11.82	5.86	3.71

Table 4

Means of Selected Variables for Banks in Different Primary Lending Strategy Groups

Primary Lending Strategy

Variable	Residential Real Estate Lenders (N=1210)	Household Lenders (N=275)	Diversified Lenders (N=931)	Business Lenders (N=620)	Business Real Estate Lenders (N=356)	Agricultural Lenders (N=698)	No-Specialty Lenders (N=219)	No Primary Strategy (N=1119)
Residential RE Loans/Assets	28.55	16.36	19.06	10.28	11.04	6.85	7.72	15.80
Consumer Installment Loans/Assets	7.94	19.15	9.09	5.28	3.71	5.12	6.35	7.43
Commercial Loans/Assets	6.78	5.71	11.05	13.91	11.00	7.74	4.80	9.51
Business RE Loans/Assets	10.86	6.87	15.76	12.64	39.72	4.53	4.60	14.34
Agricultural Loans/Assets	4.67	4.02	9.31	12.85	1.79	37.53	7.45	9.10
Retail Loans/Assets	36.58	35.09	28.30	15.72	14.85	12.14	13.98	23.32
Wholesale Loans/Assets	23.06	17.19	37.05	40.83	53.55	50.61	17.38	33.89
Loan Portfolio HHI	0.3455	0.3201	0.2725	0.2869	0.4399	0.4334	0.3049	0.2989
Total Loans/Assets	59.63	52.27	65.34	56.55	68.39	62.74	31.34	57.21
Mean Total Assets ($ 2004)	130.52	82.72	129.78	112.80	206.54	55.91	77.32	118.68
Bank Age (2004)	86.22	76.64	78.30	80.16	44.07	88.52	84.68	76.88
Number of Different Lending Strategies	1.78	2.15	2.35	2.23	2.09	1.53	1.97	3.21

Table 5

Mean Values of MEANPTROE, SDPTROE, and the Sharpe Ratio

for Banks in Each Each Primary Lending Strategy Category Controlling for Size

Primary Lending Strategy	All Sample Banks				Small Community Banks[*]				Large Community Banks[**]			
	Number	MEANPTROE	SDPTROE	Sharpe	Number	MEANPTROE	SDPTROE	Sharpe	Number	MEANPTROE	SDPTROE	Sharpe
Residential Real Estate Lenders	1210	15.07	3.77	4.14	562	13.49	4.10	3.30	648	16.45	3.48	4.87
Household Lenders	275	13.77	4.60	3.32	194	12.98	4.85	2.89	81	15.66	3.99	4.35
Diversified Lenders	931	16.11	4.54	4.00	418	14.58	5.29	3.18	513	17.36	3.93	4.67
Business Lenders	620	14.89	4.48	3.46	346	13.56	4.70	2.95	274	16.56	4.21	4.11
Business Real Estate Lenders	356	18.09	5.80	3.65	54	13.89	7.45	2.20	302	18.84	5.51	3.91
Agricultural Lenders	698	14.00	4.16	3.38	575	13.41	4.25	3.10	123	16.77	3.70	4.65
No-Specialty Lenders	219	11.32	3.52	2.60	166	10.33	3.45	2.37	53	14.42	3.73	3.29
No Primary Strategy	1119	14.60	4.92	3.39	615	12.66	5.17	2.73	584	16.65	4.65	4.08

[*]Small community banks are sample banks with total assets of $100 million or less on 12/31/2004.
[**]Large community banks are sample banks with total assets greater than $100 million and less than or equal to $1 billion on 12/31/2004.

52

Table 6

Mean Values of MEANPTROE, SDPTROE, and Sharpe Ratios

for All Sample Banks with Selected Primary Lending Strategies Controlling for Strategic Change

Primary Lending Strategy Classification

Number of Different Lending Strategies	Residential Real Estate Lenders				Household Lenders				Diversified Lenders			
	Number	MEANPTROE	SDPTROE	Sharpe	Number	MEANPTROE	SDPTROE	Sharpe	Number	MEANPTROE	SDPTROE	Sharpe
1	509	15.42	3.38	4.53	45	13.84	4.48	3.64	89	17.16	4.25	4.48
> 1	701	14.82	4.05	3.86	230	13.75	4.62	3.26	842	16.00	4.57	3.95
> 2	221	14.09	4.31	3.53	74	13.02	4.59	2.86	354	15.62	4.77	3.67

Number of Different Lending Strategies	Business Lenders				Business Real Estate Lenders				Agricultural Lenders			
	Number	MEANPTROE	SDPTROE	Sharpe	Number	MEANPTROE	SDPTROE	Sharpe	Number	MEANPTROE	SDPTROE	Sharpe
1	91	14.96	4.54	3.76	86	18.42	4.69	3.66	395	14.10	3.97	3.43
> 1	529	14.87	4.47	3.41	270	17.98	5.90	3.64	303	13.87	4.40	3.31
> 2	204	14.28	4.88	3.09	106	17.37	6.28	3.49	62	12.70	4.26	2.93

Table 7

Alternative OLS Rate of Return Regressions

Dependent Variable: MEANPTROE

Explanatory Variables	(1) COEFF	(1) T	(1) P > |t|	(2) COEFF	(2) T	(2) P > |t|	(3) COEFF	(3) T	(3) P > |t|	(4) COEFF	(4) T	(4) P > |t|
RESRED	0.39530	1.89	0.058	-0.18988	-0.79	0.431	0.01814	0.09	0.929	-0.34295	-1.46	0.145
HHD	0.94012	2.74	0.006	0.47786	1.35	0.178	0.86313	2.61	0.009	0.57427	1.67	0.096
DIVD	0.49576	2.12	0.034	0.17048	0.71	0.478	0.28865	1.31	0.190	0.08789	0.39	0.699
BUSD	0.24413	0.91	0.363	-0.16490	-0.59	0.559	0.09746	0.38	0.706	-0.15685	-0.58	0.565
BUSRED	1.21018	2.77	0.006	0.80748	1.81	0.071	1.54943	3.64	0.000	1.29115	2.96	0.003
AGD	0.15086	0.63	0.531	-0.53580	-1.92	0.054	-0.29149	-1.24	0.215	-0.71521	-2.64	0.008
NOSPLD	1.02739	2.59	0.010	0.39724	0.93	0.350	0.93239	2.28	0.023	0.53847	1.23	0.218
STATEBANK	0.60189	3.58	0.000	0.58313	3.47	0.001	0.46391	2.88	0.004	0.45439	2.82	0.005
LOGASSET	1.94487	20.94	0.000	1.93723	20.93	0.000	1.70915	18.63	0.000	1.70820	18.64	0.000
NONMATDEPR	12.37288	14.43	0.000	12.41836	14.51	0.000	12.69920	14.92	0.000	12.72241	14.96	0.000
LOANASSETR	12.76524	17.24	0.000	12.32433	16.44	0.000	14.51781	18.79	0.000	14.21244	18.08	0.000
SUBCHAPS	2.68089	17.93	0.000	2.69745	18.05	0.000	2.63689	17.93	0.000	2.64800	18.00	0.000
MBHCD	1.96069	10.95	0.000	2.00629	11.19	0.000	2.23914	12.86	0.000	2.26320	12.97	0.000
MKTSHARE	1.94292	4.65	0.000	1.85882	4.44	0.000	1.78347	4.47	0.000	1.73329	4.34	0.000
MKTDEPGR	3.23488	7.15	0.000	3.30337	7.21	0.000	3.38467	6.60	0.000	3.42520	6.61	0.000
SLMKTDEPR	-2.64774	-3.18	0.001	-2.74372	-3.29	0.001	-2.38616	-2.96	0.003	-2.45068	-3.05	0.002
NUMLENDSTRAT				-0.42112	-4.46	0.000				-0.26429	-2.88	0.004
SDPTROE							-0.34834	-11.37	0.000	-0.34264	-11.10	0.000
CONSTANT	-22.44676	-21.19	0.000	-20.76286	-18.72	0.000	-19.22561	-18.16	0.000	-18.22148	-16.58	0.000
F	158.59			149.40			160.32			151.48		
R-squared	0.3070			0.3093			0.3466			0.3476		
N	5220			5220			5220			5220		

Table 8

Alternative OLS Risk Regressions

Dependent Variable: SDPTROE

Explanatory Variables	(1) COEFF	(1) T	(1) P > |t|	(2) COEFF	(2) T	(2) P > |t|	(3) COEFF	(3) T	(3) P > |t|	(4) COEFF	(4) T	(4) P > |t|
RESRED	-1.03958	-7.04	0.000	-0.51333	-3.19	0.001	-1.03569	-7.34	0.000	-0.60401	-3.90	0.000
HHD	-0.19301	-0.74	0.459	0.23902	0.91	0.365	-0.08714	-0.35	0.724	0.26593	1.06	0.289
DIVD	-0.53495	-3.28	0.001	-0.20388	-1.24	0.214	-0.46369	-3.07	0.002	-0.19299	-1.26	0.208
BUSD	-0.22553	-1.35	0.177	0.17663	1.01	0.311	-0.09905	-0.63	0.528	0.22925	1.39	0.164
BUSRED	0.64679	2.37	0.018	0.93812	3.37	0.001	0.88836	3.31	0.001	1.12426	4.12	0.000
AGD	-1.16567	-6.00	0.000	-0.61167	-3.03	0.002	-1.12194	-6.00	0.000	-0.66799	-3.42	0.001
NOSPLD	0.04920	0.22	0.826	0.65846	2.67	0.008	0.28462	1.25	0.212	0.78143	3.14	0.002
STATEBANK	-0.34496	-3.07	0.002	-0.32934	-2.94	0.003	-0.24067	-2.31	0.021	-0.22919	-2.21	0.027
LOGASSET	-0.88261	-13.40	0.000	-0.86469	-13.18	0.000	-0.53157	-8.07	0.000	-0.52138	-7.93	0.000
LOANASSETR	2.93898	5.97	0.000	3.44448	6.79	0.000	4.41562	8.66	0.000	4.81135	9.24	0.000
EQUITYASSETR	-20.40162	-11.04	0.000	-20.25833	-11.07	0.000	-29.50839	-12.70	0.000	-29.27373	-12.71	0.000
NONINTINCR	9.19687	7.23	0.000	9.04886	7.19	0.000	10.15968	7.93	0.000	10.02587	7.89	0.000
LOANGROWTHR	0.02603	2.53	0.011	0.02230	2.31	0.021	0.01975	2.19	0.028	0.01677	1.96	0.050
LOANHERF	3.14119	5.17	0.000	3.85451	6.19	0.000	3.55554	5.52	0.000	4.13542	6.28	0.000
MBHCD	0.59343	4.99	0.000	0.56201	4.72	0.000	0.96522	8.15	0.000	0.93466	7.85	0.000
SDMKTDEPGR	3.40086	3.44	0.001	3.27599	3.30	0.001	3.32636	3.65	0.000	3.22487	3.52	0.000
NUMLENDSTRAT				0.40931	5.97	0.000				0.33580	5.16	0.000
MEANPTROE							-0.19771	-11.89	0.000	-0.19516	-11.76	0.000
CONSTANT	12.37436	14.45	0.000	10.41443	11.52	0.000	11.02325	13.33	0.000	9.43270	10.69	0.000
F	41.07			40.42			41.61			41.03		
Adj R-squared	0.1517			0.1586			0.2312			0.2358		
N	5256			5256			5256			5256		

Table 9

Alternative 2SLS Estimates of Three Simultaneous Systems

	Model A						Model B						Model C								
	Rate of Return Equation MEANPTROE Dependent			Risk Equation SDPTROE Dependent			Rate of Return Equation MEANPTROE Dependent			Risk Equation SDPTROE Dependent			Rate or Return Equation MEANPTROE Dependent			Risk Equation SDPTROE Dependent			Loan Asset Ratio Equation LOANASSETR Dependent		
Explanatory Variables	COEFF	T	P > |t|	COEFF	T	P > |t|	COEFF	T	P > |t|	COEFF	T	P > |t|	COEFF	T	P > |t|	COEFF	T	P > |t|	COEFF	T	P > |t|
RESRED	1.10411	4.02	0.000	-1.03056	-7.22	0.000	0.11566	0.39	0.694	-0.55871	-3.59	0.000	-0.00752	-0.03	0.979	-0.54724	-3.46	0.001	0.00758	1.24	0.214
HHD	1.07864	2.51	0.012	-0.21659	-0.88	0.381	0.27589	0.62	0.535	0.17159	0.69	0.493	1.25379	2.80	0.005	0.24938	0.88	0.377	-0.05909	-6.40	0.000
DIVD	0.88530	2.96	0.003	-0.49555	-3.18	0.001	0.33613	1.11	0.267	-0.19986	-1.27	0.203	-0.69952	-1.95	0.051	-0.28300	-1.30	0.194	0.06101	11.55	0.000
BUSD	0.51296	1.57	0.115	-0.15847	-0.99	0.324	-0.18949	-0.56	0.575	0.20356	1.22	0.224	0.14602	0.45	0.655	0.23510	1.31	0.190	-0.02126	-3.46	0.001
BUSRED	0.55129	1.08	0.281	0.82004	3.05	0.002	-0.18854	-0.35	0.725	1.08359	3.96	0.000	-0.82415	-1.65	0.099	0.96347	2.74	0.006	0.03776	4.07	0.000
AGD	0.98126	3.12	0.002	-1.17285	-6.24	0.000	-0.17851	-0.52	0.601	-0.67473	-3.46	0.001	-0.93438	-2.56	0.011	-0.73485	-3.42	0.001	0.04667	7.08	0.000
NOSPLD	1.20341	2.82	0.005	0.19384	0.85	0.394	0.10795	0.23	0.816	0.74344	3.01	0.003	4.25018	4.33	0.000	1.09975	1.57	0.116	-0.24407	-27.78	0.000
STATEBANK	0.86181	4.11	0.000	-0.27289	-2.56	0.011	0.84235	3.99	0.000	-0.25581	-2.41	0.016	0.47347	2.20	0.028	-0.29076	-2.33	0.020	0.02506	6.71	0.000
LOGASSET	2.39454	19.02	0.000	-0.68979	-8.60	0.000	2.40473	19.03	0.000	-0.66959	-8.40	0.000	1.83178	9.61	0.000	-0.71393	-6.80	0.000	0.03061	13.08	0.000
NONMATDEPR	11.71038	12.02	0.000				11.75781	12.01	0.000				14.67424	13.88	0.000						
LOANASSETR	9.43424	9.45	0.000	3.79890	6.98	0.000	8.48606	8.14	0.000	4.26915	7.72	0.000	26.06985	6.49	0.000	5.76454	2.07	0.039			
SUBCHAPS	2.76973	15.98	0.000				2.80290	16.06	0.000				2.70381	16.35	0.000						
MBHCD	1.44439	6.41	0.000	0.79752	6.28	0.000	1.49658	6.61	0.000	0.77314	6.07	0.000	1.36176	6.56	0.000	0.72311	4.49	0.000			
MKTSHARE	2.22664	4.34	0.000				2.09492	4.04	0.000				3.01317	5.66	0.000				0.03433	1.97	0.049
MKTDEPGR	2.94367	6.18	0.000				3.04846	6.42	0.000				2.39588	4.57	0.000						
SLMKTDEPR	-3.14867	-3.17	0.002				-3.34376	-3.32	0.001				-3.76161	-3.95	0.000						
EQUITYASSETR				-25.79956	-11.06	0.000				-25.76417	-11.14	0.000				-23.53495	-5.05	0.000			
NONINTINCR				9.76419	7.59	0.000				9.63995	7.56	0.000				9.78376	7.42	0.000			
LOANGROWR				0.02313	2.37	0.018				0.01973	2.15	0.032				0.01815	1.94	0.053			
LOANHERF				3.25754	5.29	0.000				3.89911	6.17	0.000				3.92642	6.23	0.000			
SDMKTDEPGR				2.91347	3.14	0.002				2.78506	2.99	0.003				2.58714	2.51	0.012			
NUMLENDSTRAT	0.66385	6.64	0.000				-0.73856	-5.89	0.000	0.36682	5.61	0.000	-0.28704	-1.77	0.077	0.40524	4.26	0.000	-0.02630	-11.63	0.000
SDPTROE							0.69858	6.97	0.000				0.34764	2.48	0.013				0.02083	10.30	0.000
MEANPTROE				-0.11282	-4.01	0.000				-0.11489	-4.10	0.000				-0.10263	-3.04	0.002			
CONSTANT	-28.56581	-19.20	0.000	11.75172	13.71	0.000	-25.93469	-17.72	0.000	9.97438	11.07	0.000	-30.27505	-19.93	0.000	9.12962	4.90	0.000	0.18713	5.88	0.000
F	119.14			40.41			111.52			39.98			103.71			37.96			250.94		
N	5218			5218			5218			5218			5218			5218			5218